2016

To Diane,
seeing the extraordinary
in the ordinary...
Kate Falvey

the language *of* little girls

the language *of* little girls

POEMS

Kate Falvey

David Robert Books

Published by David Robert Books
P.O. Box 541106
Cincinnati, OH 45254-1106

Book design by M Kellner

ISBN: 9781625491930

Poetry Editor: Kevin Walzer
Business Editor: Lori Jareo

Visit us on the web at www.davidrobertbooks.com

For my grandmother, Laura, my mother, Elaine,
and my daughter, Annie

contents

The Language of Little Girls

I.

God is a project
cut out in foil
and pressed into paste
on dark red paper. He
will stick there forever,
shining in one of his guises:
a tall thin cross with a clever
tilt of halo at its top, crayoned
in a brilliant stroke of yellow and
stuck like a derby, rakishly over
a mass of invisible thorns.
In the chest of the cross a fury of
orange flames is gathered together like
a wild-flower posy and the orange is
forced hard to get the fury in and to
make the orange show up on the red.
Tiger-lilies are the shapes of the flames and
this is o.k. because God is known
to enjoy his lilies. Hosannas are
at His feet. They are chubby and puffed
and stunted in pink attitudes of glee. They have
horns instead of rattles and they make a fat
harsh invisible noise like babies squalling
into gurgles. They are cut from Christmas
cards which is a testament for God since the wings
are very difficult to pink and to my knowledge
only two tiny fronds were sheered but none of
the toes, thank God, though they curled impossibly.
This God will be a bookmark and won,
more than likely by Danny Mulcahy, who I love,
in a bee.

God is a two-way mirror and the
seeing eyes of nuns. The mirror is

any wall, even the air. There is no place,
even under the covers when it storms, even in
the candid dark of the confessional, or behind
the playfield where Maureen and I make secrets
that He doesn't x-ray vision into. He could
see your bones and your wishes. He could see
your nails curving into claws and the jumps
you would make, and the snarls, if you lived
like a stealthy black shadow in a tree. He could see
even what you didn't do — if He had mind to
focus you in His scanner which
you never know when He might. And, really, in a way
He is like a fly because His eyes are
many little worlds, kaleidoscopes ever rounding with
the fruit of the whole of Space.
I don't think He sees in the
regular way. I stare for a long time at a
cherry and it does seem to make ripe
atoms of itself and the atoms do a little
dance and are paler than
the cherry, more like a blush veil with a night-
blue feathered in and then the atoms start to swell
and swivel and they become all the things of this world:
goats and cradles and grapes and my grandpa and darning
needles over lily pads in the greeny brake of Tonetta Lake. Then
like wavering flatworms or angelic banners heralding over
the creche, the atoms mean something different
and signal their change in glow and elongation. They
matter now as song and things that can't be touched
like lies and meanness and the sharing of
cherry tomatoes with Danny Mulcahy and the taste
all the way through you after a dinner of chicken and
buttered spinach. It isn't now the act
that the atoms are but the cave in the act where
the feelings whirl and then they are the very
feelings themselves which have no way to say them
because if you say *sad* there is not just a plain sad that

makes the same movement in the world. You feed feeling and
seeing to the world and the world keeps
being made. The sad when Cindy says
I sing like opera and not like shows is very
different from the sad when Daddy kisses Cindy
goodnight and she is not even
his child. This is also very different from
the peculiar sad when the monitors
Leonard and Danny
chalked Pat Hines' name on the
mantis-colored green of the board
to report her for talking when
she didn't even peep and this
was just because Pat Hines was
bigger than girls and wore small plaid bows
clipped to her jagged dark hair and because
Sister said she was a slow learner but
there was no way she talked and so
Danny and Leonard should not have
put her on the talkers' list
and when Pat cried redly with
snivels and no tissues
because Sister had a voice like a thousand crows
and she punished by making you a dunce,
Maureen and I could not stand it anymore and we
leapt up and astonished every eye by flying
out of our seats and winging Pat with our protection
and I said, even though I loved Danny and Leonard played
the violin, which made even nuns clap, I said,
"You better write my name, too, because now you have
someone who really talked" and Maureen said,
"Me, too" and everyone was just gaga with
wildness and our names went up and then
a dozen names flurried that couldn't be caught up with
in script and then someone, maybe Barbara Schul, wheezed
"Sister's coming!" and everything died down fast like the
still and topple of fifty crazy wind-up toys.

Our names vanished from the board, and we all
had our hands laced on our desks when Sister
strode in, suspecting. The monitors were pets and so
when she quizzed them on our goodness they confirmed
our quiet and the blurry rasures under the Talkers heading
never even gave us away.
My heart slapped like paddles killing water snakes
and I brought nonpareils for Richard Armstrong ever after.

All of these sads are a lot like mads and may be
bad examples. Mad is a sin
that we don't
discuss. The priest has to hear of it
and you can bet God
figures it out.

The atoms know this. When they shift
again they make soft energy
like faintly rosy steam
the color of kneecaps after a long kneel,
and I can see into the very insides of
angels and I know God's sigh is the
voice of all the world.
Then there's just the cherry again
bobbing on its stem. When I
bite it I think I am
eating the heads of angels and
the strange tongued world of
whatever all
there is.

II.
I was a worker bee and Maureen was the Queen.
She had a scepter and her throne was downy
with quilted purple cushions. Her antennae
were foiled in gold and when the drones
skulked in with hefted heels and bowie knives

raised and ready to spear and they
stomped among the bonnets of the
mewling little larvae and threatened the
industry of the whole hive I
didn't much care but when
one particularly repugnant and
cowardly drone fizzed up to the
Queen in his jacket of furred stripes and
savagely bent her antenna which was
a pipe cleaner and so was
bait for easy twisting, I
wanted to sling in a fury of swarm
all of my catapulting menace and
sting him with sticks and stones and
all of my gnashing bee teeth and
lunatic bee punches
but this was not
in the plot.

I slept in Maureen's bed,
our hair vined together in
early summer Irish, the early
dark pinked in fluttering warbles of
maple leaf and new gold.

Her tall sisters were as beautiful as she,
especially Kathleen, whose forehead shone with
broad pellucid whiteness, her kind eyes
blue as dreams as she helped me to
my meat. I was stunned with so much
new and dumbly forgot how to slice and so
Kathleen cut my roast beef with gentle,
unobtrusive efficiency, just like a
storybook mother, and no one, not even the tall
father, who had mild eyes like Kathleen's,
made me feel like a
spectacle

because my manners were so
babyish and because I couldn't
move or talk
normally.

I hadn't known foreheads
could be beautiful. And I couldn't believe
that Maureen had such fairy
princess sisters, such a freckled,
smiling mother, and a father who
reminded me of mine but who
joked with his daughters and chucked them
under their chins and patted his wife happily
like he did this all the time.

In the morning Maureen kissed me awake
and whispered
"Wake up, Sleeping Beauty"
and everything
even the pancakes
became achingly
enchanted.

III.
Families I did not know
troubled vacantly into the pews
and turned to mark the censer's swing,
mechanical and raled,
the advancing swath of incense
mordant and important,
a restless, fumy palliative of dire,
insistent worth.

Mantillas and prim afterthoughts of
hankies snowed frailly from the women's
bowed heads. A few
pillboxes in pink straw perched
absently,

without intending irreverence.
And the men in grey
and black and blue shifted
in their buffed shoes and
red hands shook hugely
with the strain of their
juddering grace. We
collected like feathers in a draft
against the coffin, grim and
moonish in our
communion clothes, tucked
organdy and serge nervously shying
the mahogany. How
could Robert Reuss be
in that trunk with God
when only Wednesday he
was missing the spelling of
immaculate and flicking up the
plaid hem of Eileen Haskell's skirt?
How could we
let the boys grabble again
in the play yard when
the sun had one less shadow
of a teasing hand?

And it just wasn't
true anymore
that the fingers
on the Jesus baby moved
in mischievous communion
or that His polished mother
wept a pearly piety
of tears.

IV.
In the vestibule before the
locked glass door,

the apple blossoms belling and
beseeching in the yard,
Maureen and I
lifted shirts
and showed chests
to compare the slight muzzy
russet of mine and
the perfect
pink plane of her not yet starting
the hurt

Malady/The Glory of Little Girls

I had a guardian angel
as a child. She was pert
and blonde and she rode
on the handlebars of my
blue two-wheeler to keep me
from being conspicuously
alone. Her hair was short
and fine and I watched the
fair fringe of it flicker
on her neck as I steered us
through a nagging derision of
unfamiliar streets, my new
neighborhood reluctantly entered
and browsed
with the noncommittal ire
of the choiceless.
Boys with no names
swung at our wheels
and, sturdily noncombatant, we
rose on the speed of our own
hearts' pedaling
into the treed and brambled sward
in the crotch of the

fork in the road.

Here there were toadstools
and tiny spotted frogs and
alley cats foraging for unlicked bones
far from the chaste yards
of lunch-scraps, cardinals, and squirrels,
a dish of cream scrupled
by the kitchen door,
a routine chase and ravening
of a gusted seed-pod or

easy grounded wren.
Here, in a rough angle of
brush and bracken
pocketed between ways home
cats could be feral again
and cost
abundant lives.

The Language of Little Girls: Doll-Babies

Connie's pink gingham is slightly bedraggled.
Marilyn's bubble-sleeved organza is prickly with starch.
We play nurses and treat their wounds.
Behind the brick house is a dense thicket of nettles and trash.
We a stomp a clearing in the scrub and lay planks
from the being-built new buildings
into the shape of a laying-down house.
We filch real peeled-off shingles to patch
the triangle of our roof. We weigh the roof down with stones
and section our rooms with lines of pebbles and grit.
Hunched in the bedroom, we splay Connie and Marilyn
on a bed of rough mulch and wings of fern which
Mrs. Dawson would flip if she knew we scooped and tore.
Connie has a head wound and Marilyn hurt her spine.
We dot rashy zigzags and pulpy clots of blood with blood
from our own scraped ankles and shins onto the blushing
rubber of their girly skins. Then we are priests dishing out
atonements for all their ragged, prissy sins.

The Terrible Miss Terrell

She was, in P.S. 103, the tyrant of 3-K.
Miss D. looked starched and pre-arranged
with her brusque flannel slacks
and studied frowns, doling out symmetrical
rounds of yellow dough for us to lump into
cheery Christmas ashtrays. Yet she was
no match for Miss T, who looked the perfect
picture book grandma: spectacles and frizzled hair,
and pleated floral skirts outspread with what might have been
a bountiful lap. If she wasn't secretly a ghoul.

The girls
could play in the wooden half-house,
the back cut away so we couldn't get stuck.
The boys could play with wooden blocks,
but not the girls.
If you inched too close to the border of the boys,
Miss T. would snatch you back and stuff you
in a corner, where Miss D. would lurk
and shame you into tears. Miss T., as anyone could see,
controlled Miss D.'s direction. Miss D.
said "naughty, naughty" and made you
wash your hands, and caught you doing things
you didn't know you did
but that you did.
Miss T., however, pinched each day
into sticky traps in which
only naughty happened
and caught you doing things
you didn't know you did,
and didn't.

Antiphon

A gaffe once
when I salted my
cream of wheat. We had
a shaker for sugar
in my house and the
salt was
a natural
mistake. Papa's
summer house smelled like
screen doors slamming
and rain tipped
out of green metal porch chairs
and cool slate floors and close
maple dining-table talk and
white plates of rare tomatoes
sliced with olive oil and oregano
and strawberries and vermouth
and circlets of mesh warning the
frogs out of the drains.

Papa called me stupid
and cowed my mother
when she tried
to explain.

He wasn't an unkind man
and he'd never said
an unkind thing
to me before.
He took me down to the water's edge,
untied the boat, and rowed me into
the far-side lilies
in the dearest diminishment
of light. He built
this house

himself and sweated in
his tee-shirt carving shapes
in the front-yard firs. He
pressed wine in the chilly cellar
and let me watch him
fill the jugs. He rigged a

tire-swing for me and made
play pipes out of twigs and acorns. He
found safe mushrooms growing and
knew a wild hike to a clear secret stream
that you would work hard to get to,
breaking through troubles of sweetbriers
and bottle flies, oak burls, burdocks,
midges, and heat
just to dip your thirsty hands
and drink.

Foodstuffs

So when Mama's apron is on crooked,
duck. Try to warm myself
with wall and dust motes.
Bars of early evening light
close off the fire escape
and I am one shudder away from
total stillness,
one missing ingredient away from
flaring into spectacular sight.

The pot lids shut in thunder.
Her fist is buried in the sticky dough.
Then, before I even hear the shush
of her apron as she spins,
she yanks me to my feet, flour erupting
as I crack against the blue-rimmed bowl.
You. Tell him
I need salt I need milk I need oil I need eggs.
IOU. I need bones for the soup. I need
whatever he can give. Salt milk oil eggs
Bones with still a little meat,
the stingy bastard. Tell him no tricks.
Tell him IOU again
your father.

She rights her apron with a ghastly tug,
marks time with her wooden spoon.
I slink to the door, clutching peril
like a threadbare cloak.

On the street, the air tastes metal,
like my lost roller skate key.
I dawdle, I skulk, I try to become deliberate
as need, but I am reedy as the last cry
of a long-starved cat and unequal

to the grown up stares that lie in wait,
withholding. But Mama waits
so I slip dumbly into the grocer's,
shy against the counter, invoking St. Jude
as I wait.

For supper we have soup with noodles
and eggs with potatoes.
Mama ladles Daddy's bowl brimful
but she pours me extra milk and sneaks
a lump of sugar beneath my bread and oleo.

The Poetics of Character: Solitude and Attention

A child
must spend
hours alone watching
a snail, confident
that when the wind blows
the snail will
snuggle in its feelers
and belong to its groove of soil,
a dark swag of cabbage
breaking the westering squall.

A child
must right
the woozy stalks
of iris and calendula,
even against nature,
and for a damp demented time,
in vain, and then
heap the purpled spoilings
into feed for future bracings,
spry and hopeful rallyings
against resilient storms.

A child
must trouble
to resist
lazing by the lucid brook
when hoe-rills must be struck
and small stones routed into paths
or when the frills of coming chicory
need daubing against blight
and the snap beans staking
in aspiration of
their striving.

A child
must laze
by the brook
and not do another
blessed thing
except feel
the chill of the bank
and the wild suppositions
in the dozy spirals of
the mind.

A child
must be called
to supper.

Girls Girls Girls

I. By the Sea

We know it, instinctively.
The tide has turned and our mouths, agape,
scrape the moon-damp sand, like bluefish stunned
while feeding on menhaden or meaty strips of clam
or crab, chummed in thin streaks on waves elate with blood.
Hooked dumb and pressed beneath the hunters' thumbs
and bootsoles, we toss and squirm as if we had a ghost
of a chance. Spent, resistless, we spit out bits of sea wrack
and ruin, lay flat and let them
angle in for kills and kills and kills.

Exquisite pinks from translucent filmy shells
line our tongues. We
will never speak of it again.

II. Giving Chase

A rapture of pine needles
and all I want to steal
is dust.

There were so many rocks
by the curbside, though memory
mounts them in multiples, gemmy
and pulsing with fairy-dawn light.
A breed of little girls in wilted cotton shorts
and sandals, red-faced with the sparks
of quartz, heedless in the thrumming joy
of smashing, smashing, smashing
piles of crystalline guts.

III. What's Left

A filmy little giggle by the wayside,
a husk of sandal-shaped coral washed up
on someone else's dimly dreamy shore.

Queens Homily: Mrs. Dawson and Mrs. New

Mrs. Dawson, as tall as a strong-backed man and as hard,
lifts her ruddy hands to tug some reeling fruit from a windy green
    September.
Her white hair wisps and blows from the red borders of her
    kerchief
like the wayward parachutes of the dandelions she
scares me into wishing on in secret.
Her head grazes the last branches of the ancient
Lady apple tree as she angles into a hollow and twists
to beat the squirrels.

I do not know if her face is kind or not.

She will give my mother a basket of apples
And tonight we will have a cake called *kuchen*
and my father will ask why don't we just have pie,
American, with dips of vanilla ice cream.

Erect Mrs. Dawson comes with Mrs. New, who is curved
like the back of a pale-skinned peach.
Mrs. New reaches just above
Mrs. Dawson's checkered apron strings;
she looks like a kind of old-lady luggage,
over-packed and bobbling
by Mrs. Dawson's long side as they
hang their special suet cakes on wires
for the chickadees and sparrows.
Mrs. New has tiny straight white hair
that fans onto her powdery neck in frilly streaks
and eyes like overcast June country skies.
She leads me to the piano in the cellar, like an
explorer homing in on buried treasure.
The wooden stairs are painted creaky black
and Mrs. New's two handed grip
on the red banister makes the downward struggle

slow enough for me to spy the hint
of milky yellow in her little spikes of hair.

Mrs. Dawson stands in the red kitchen at the top of the stairs,
and squints at me accusingly.

We land on the cement
and Mrs. New judders up to pull a cord for light.
She is just below me in height,
but it is her expedition.
I am not in charge of bringing light
or choosing what to touch.
The cellar is another country. It smells sudsy —
warm with dust and difference.
I am too shy to ask what is hidden in the boxes
or what whiteness billows
from the splintered tops of
wicker crates, or what glistens
red and palest brown and green
in rows of jars on thick gray wooden shelves.

I would push into the wilderness
of aprons, socks, and blouses
drying on racks and overhead ropes
because there is no sun today
and washing must go on. I would up-end the
farthest trunk and pore over lore from the
ragged shores of *Hungary*, a lopsided world
of heavy eyelids, shoes, and skillets,
heavy tongues keeping children from the roses,
cakes heavy with sugar and tart apples.

Mrs. New crooks her crooked fingers and
we sit on the here and now bench —
waxy black and a bit wobbly —
or maybe I am wobbly
in Mrs. New's company.

Her dress is peach with tiny rucks and pleats
and pearly bodice buttons
and a pattern of blue posies
tied into fans with swirling ribbons.

Mrs. New nods to me.
I tap a key and tense at the sudden sound.
Her hands are curled and won't flatten out
so she loosens a startling music out of the stillness
with unsplayed fingers. I don't think it's a real song
but I am surprised by its dainty prettiness.

Matty and Hatty and the L-Seven Marauders
or *Wooly Bully* in the Moonlight

We said, *Dance, Hell!* You think
a bit of shimmy shake, some rotgut wine,
some stompin' on the sawdust of disaster
is all we have in mind? You know
nothin' 'bout real women. We
are ridin' out on sheer
memory of flame,
ornery, unbraced, and
movin' like near thunder in the moon-arrested sky,
the branches quaking shadowy warnings,
the owls slinking in the leaves. The dull thud of the
hairy hooves, jiving 'round the fire, the smoky
incantations swiveling up over our loosened braids and
breasts. *Hot Damn!* Matty commented
when the horns glittered between trails of moss and mischief.
Someone's being sacrificed tonight. Light the stage! And
then the seven sisters advanced from the creeping cauldron smoke
and drew us bodily in, opening flickering arms,
flashing chips of mirrored moonshine
to admit us to the circle. The last thing I heard
was my own voice cawing:
Matty, we've got to
take a chance.
Someone rasped out the numbers and our names.
Then the wool was pulled over our eyes
and we — presto-change-o — learned
to do the same.

Alice and Red at the O.K. Corral

I.

Alice makes her exit
and drags the tidy summer's day
into the brush.
A close call, skirts lifting
in the looming cave, the sheer nerve
of her descent providing a
counter-weight to the necessary
blunder of her fall. The animals
breathe with ridiculous dimension.
One false move, and she's done for,
bunnies be damned. Who can trust a
shape-shifter? Even a fool girl knows
to keep away from beasts marking time.

II.

Red takes cover under a kindly death cap,
grabs a frilly ankle as Alice swishes, planless,
through the tears. "Where are you off to?"
Red asks, offering a wary seedcake from her store.

"I think I was off to see a wizard, but that may
have been another someone else
in another nevermore. Who
are you?"

"I'm daughter to my mother and
granddaughter to
my grandmother.
I'm not to leave the trail
but the roots tripped me up
and before I could
upright myself, I lurched into this covert where
everyone talks and no one knows their name."
"I am not the same, but I recall that I am Alice

27

and I have a cuddly cat and I was cool
and moony in the shade just a tiny while ago.
Did you see a vested rabbit
dashing madly, watching with a shiny fob?"

I saw
a wolf.
He asked me for the time and grinned. I
am not a snob nor impolite
but I didn't like his tone. I
tossed my head, said,
'I want to be alone!' then
soared away, my cape full of flight
and red alertness,
and broke into this copse.
A caterpillar told me
to stay put.
Until I should move again.
Or until I should be moved."

III.
High noon and the bullets blaze.
The girls huddle and withstand the threat
of assistance from the law. A face-off of lead and claw.
The silver one is meant for girlish dreams.

Running with Wolves

They adopt me when my hair
distinguishes itself from the sedge,
my arms relieved of summer mosses.
A trickle of light tells them my tear
is not a fleck of ice melt on the petal
of a cloudberry.

Thompson Street

So you are arrived.
Dad and the boys
thunder up the stairs
with the heavy work
of your new self.
There is a chalky pink lamp
fanned into a shell-shape, an
edgy thick pine table that
already looks beaten to its pulp,
mother-made gingham curtains
to hide the doorless bathroom,
and a cobalt bowl scooped into a swan
to catch whatever light the skinny fifth floor windows toss.

On his way up, Dad says to each tiny lady on
each tiled landing: "This is my daughter. This is my
daughter. This is my daughter." They nod
in Italian. They know the code. *Watch her.*
She is a good girl. She is my good girl. Watch her.
Keep her safe.

I.
Charlie accuses, "My God!
It's like a little home!" Because you
painted the cabinets a slick mauve
and hung the needlework roses from
the Canal Street flea above Papa's bookcase
and made sure that the floating gold of your mother's
sheer curtains was tied back with rippley lace. Because
you made your bed with a pastel patchwork quilt
and snuggled a child's black chair into the corner to
hold your thrift store hats. Because Nanny's
desk was painted blue and had small drawers to
hold your typing paper, ribbons, and stamps. Because
Grandma's rocking chair was re-covered

in a cranberry Liberty print and angled
conversationally toward the husky futon.
You had some nerve for culling
the working class oddments shifted to you
and making them into your ardently picturesque own.
You had some nerve for nesting,
and scaring all the boys around for miles.

II.
The clipping in the built-in bed
told of a disease
gay men were getting a lot of.
The clipping was small and creased
and not from the front page.
Dad said the bed looked simple
enough to disassemble, that he was
glad I had my own mattress.

III.
Mrs. C. on two
says I shouldn't worry
about the bugs. If
I am clean and wash my dishes
right away and don't leave
crumbs or snack wrappers
on the table, and if I wipe
up spills and shower water
quickly, then the bugs will
go pester someone dirty.
"You are a clean girl, I know.
I see your father when you come.
So don't worry. You not gonna
have no problem."
I don't tell her that I sometimes
can't help leaving unwashed
cups clogged with milky tea
and bowls rimmed with flecks

of sauce and cheese in the
Lilliputian sink, that sometimes
I sit and stare for hours at a time.

IV.
The men are all thick
and dapper in tweedy
overcoats and shiny black shoes.
There are five of them, I think,
but I know not to look too hard.
They stop talking as I swing through
the lobby and dissolve up the stairs.
"Hello," the stockiest one
squints his scary eyes into a make-shift smile.
The others just watch me, affectless and stiff.
One uncrosses his arms as I pass.
I smile as girlishly as I can and flood
the stairwell with adrenaline, the way
I used to when tumbling up from the basement
as a child, especially if my parents weren't home.

Later, Mary and I giggle
over the gangsters in our neighborhood,
and agree that they help to purge the streets
of less gentlemanly thugs.
Mrs. Ferrugi snarls. "They can turn like that.
You pay them respect, they leave you alone."
Mrs. C. says never to look them in the eyes.

V.
The scratching sound is coming from the window.
It can't be a bird. It is too slanty sounding,
like something dragging, not pecking.
The night before you got tipped out of a taxi
and poured like a bucket of elvers into a river
of spumy darkness, then you barely watched yourself
writhe up too many shivering,

fogbound stairs. Mrs. C.'s peery pouchy eyes
are part of the dim recall of the upward journey.
The scratching sound has you noticing that
you are still in your clothes — a velvet bolero
with rhinestone buttons, a frothy grey muddle of
tiered scallops for a skirt, black stockings with a
ghostly diamond pattern, now mostly rucked and split.
You look around for your hat — a flirty black cloche of
felt and feathers and vaguely recall flinging it
at a derelict drummer, when a startle of small hand
snakes through the curtains and a face blends
into the folds of the dank afternoon. Just as swiftly,
it spies you, and flees. You lay for a long while,
breathing in the sordid taste of your own inertia,
not ready to face the narrow escape of
the rent in the grime-ridden screen.

VI.
The best cancer hospital is right uptown.
It's convenient to have a daughter with a fold out bed
and no need to talk
about the future

204th Street

I.

I might have made up Tony Ice,
but Tony Shoe, Tony Tailor
were on the block and real.
Whoever sold the ices — Vinnie? Frankie?
Angelo? Joe? — was next to Tony Shoe
and lemon was my choice when Grandma
let us go with a curt fistful of nickels,
her head looming from the window
like a salt-wracked figurehead on a proud Bronx prow.
Ice melted in the pleats of the paper cup and sweetness
creased into the least press of pulp as Grandma peered
between wrinkles and the rails of the fire escape
and waved us homeward with a flick
of her wooden spoon.

II.

Josie's place had pink bubble gum shaped like catcher's mitts
and Crows and Charms and Dots and Sugar Babies,
lanky Sugar Daddies on sticks and glass jars of mints
and butterscotch and sours. She
had white spun-sugar hair and kind crinkly eyes and she
let me have two of anything I spied.
She was a cousin, the precise lineage obscure but effective,
resulting in my gratis sweets and solitude
as Grandma, settled on a tall red stool,
paid me little mind while I leaned
into the talk, far-off and familiar,
of the elders,
words warm and swirling
in the vanilla-infused air.
Che cosa state facendo?
Ma-donâ
vaffanculo!

I sat at the marble counter and played with my stash:
two cozy mary janes boxing in the sassy blue mints
and the pixie sticks making a fence for
the root beer barrel horses to vault over
and escape the cowboy Sugar Daddy wranglers.
The catcher's mitt gum was an entity, too perfect to chew.
Its smooth pinkie-tip-sized palm could hold

one lick, one glistening cherry jujube
and the voice of my Grandma
forever.

III.
So the clothes are on the line cooling as the evening falters.
The strong sun is almost over and the sheets will be furled in,
much bleached, no longer crisp, but smelling reassuringly
of brick dust, the sassing of the courtyard children, and
all the greetings pitched from ledge to ledge
as the building's women hang their clothes.
I play with the macaroni cutter on the floor,
running its frilly wheel around the
scrubbed grey linoleum, pretending
it is a fancy silver and red car. I run
it near Grandma's legs, which have nylons on
even though it's summer, while she stands
and stirs at the stove. She sings in a voice
like heavy pearls swinging in twilight
on the breast of a movie star.

IV.
There are dozens of cats in the alley
between worlds.
The backs of the other buildings
are as remote as a land beyond the sea,
strange and alluring.
Grandma's bedroom window is a forbidden zone.
I can peer but not lean and the cats,

skulking around trash cans, glower and swat,
wafting bony orange tails.

Cats haunt the sugar of the streets,
snarl in pearly whispers, kneading nightfall.
The soft dark yields to my leaning
then quickly anneals as my Grandma's voice
of warning hauls me back inside.

Shadows follow me to the tall mirror
that dips like a moon into the valley
of the heavy vanity.
Inside the slope of the vanity's secret ebony box
is a stash of old painted doll furniture:

an icebox, a sofa, a piano, a chair.
I tilt them to the window and invite a
menagerie of tiny winged cats
to sit, to play, to *mangi*.

V.
The bed is spread with rows of white cloths
laid out with just-cut noodles.
The bed is so high, it is hard to get up to see
so I try vaulting the curving mahogany footboard
while Grandma dices onions for the gravy.
The tomatoes plunk into the pot, the oil sizzles
to crescendo. I can hear
the kitchen, a blur of clinks and smells and promise,
Grandma's lacy whistling swirling the steamy air.

Then her arm surrounds me, yanks me down
a peg or two
from the bedstead,
my bones like a bag of walnuts, clattering,
though I'd swear I can still hear her
whistling *Torna a Surriento*
in the kitchen.

204th Street: Almond Cake

A little cup of tea.
A little piece of cake. What do I eat?
I scramble an egg. No more.
Who's to cook
for? I don't wanna eat — I got
my coffee in the morning with
my paper. I can still see, Thank God,
but some days my eyes ache. Where
do I go? My bones
are weak. The streets — I don't know
nobody no more. Who's
left? I got
Pakistanis across the hall.
Two little girls —
Nasreen and Saba — their mother
I don't see.
They call me Grandma. Big eyes,
big pests.
I don't know
about the older one, but that little Saba is
too much. "Grandma, make me some
meatball. Grandma, I like you cook" —
They came the first time when I had
my Carmine here — how long ago was that? —
I made some sauce.
Those kids smelled it in the halls and came
sniffing. Carmine said,
These *mulinyans*. They steal. They
mooch. I had plenty,
so what? I dipped
some bread and gave them
each a meatball. Now they come
from school, do their homework. I help
them with their English. Saba is
a whip. The other is too lazy so I say,

You. You gonna come to my house,
you gotta do your English. You do
your school, or you no get a *scarola* soup.
Madonna mia, my own grandkids don't
eat this soup. My own grandkids don't
come by. These Pakistanis, they
beg me, Grandma, scaro, scaro — So cute.

Their house stinks with some kind of spice
I don't know. Who the hell
could eat a stink
like that? The mother
wears some dark veil
like a nun. Like a little *melanzana*. Like the old ladies
of St. Lucy's when I was a girl on 1-0-6 and Second.
She brought me an almond cake — a nice round
yellow cake with powdered sugar sprinkled on.
Thank you, she shoved the plate at me.
Teach. Nasreen, Saba. Teach.
Grandma. You eat.
I had just a sliver with my coffee.
A little too coarse.
A little rough, grainy.
Maybe too sweet, she got too much
sugar in the mix. But not bad — and a lot like one I
used to make before I got
too old to beat the eggs.

In Kitty Liffey's Bar and Grill, Last Round
(after Radiohead's "How to Disappear Completely")

The streets are ablaze with wind and mayhem,
something fishy and tidal looming toward the dawn.
At the edge of the pier, the glassy eyed barkeep
calls for final rounds. There is protest in the air.
A voice like muffled fireworks sputtering over dampened
dreams uncoils from the juke. Two girls do a muggy
shimmy by the door, fizzing noxious laughter. The newly
coupled coo and arch, preparing for immanent
disaster. Loners stall in groups, still courting time,
dodging the pent heavens, the skeletal lightning, the
eerie marrow of the riven night.
I am the only one here
who is not here
and though I am lowering
and elemental, and I know my way around
a coming storm, when I unspool from my
corner stool and float toward the open door,
the light foams from the mouth of the dark and
I haven't a ghost
of a chance.

Notes for a Ghost Poem

Old Lady Lightning
This can't be right.
No one told me there were fissures —
bracts of bright attention in a
gently meditative dark.

Lakes, serene and deadly,
and I, in my trails of organdy and frills,
am chilled with my own sneaky laughter.

Mama said, no. Step onto the path and
don't annoy the flagstones. Keep still
and let your veil do all the talking. Do not let
your glance disturb the air or
someone will know you have eyes.

And the stiff plight of your shoulders is a
dead giveaway.

If you mark your trail with crumbs,
laments, or birdseed, it is likely that you
will supply the mouths for miles around
with stealth, intent, and nerve.

Once there was a fountain misting
into the twilight. Now there is a stone fin
in the woods, scales mossy and lichenous
and the cracked back of a tail cresting
through swells of blackened leafmold.

Lucy, do you hear me? Lucy, I'm calling.

I'm here in the snow. By the window.
In the snow.

Better yet, steer clear of the summer house.
You know what happens there, don't you?
Don't you, don't you,
you credulous little fool?

Ghost Poem

I. Out of Season

Flutter and snap.
Ice in the drinks
and a lavender sachet, past romance,
all shivered netting,
its brittle husks of Hidcote,
making perpetual grit in the undies.

Her giddy laughter.

II. Surrender

Glad rags —
really raggy —
on the prowl,
a mess of laddered tights and frizzy silks,
fringes predatory and draggling
in the mothy light
as if, really, there was something
to gain or
to hide.

Treat me like a lady,
the reddest lips command.
A tricky plank on the pier distends.
The strand leaks crushed mollusks and
footfalls. A trail of vaporous scarf betides
another scrape or elision,
the grungy mottled silk
scavenging the driftwood
for anything that moves.

Cora on the Beach

She shook
out the feathers
like they
were her own,
plucked
from iridescent wing
or tail or
breast
and stuck
them willy nilly
on an odd
chunk of graying wood —
indelicate,
asymmetrical, which is to say,
hefty,
clunky, rough, and rotten.
The glue
made its own edgy whorls,
glistered
brown and imprudently caked;
the
feathers couldn't be everywhere; this
wasn't
about birds
though she
could just
glimpse flocks of kingfishers
or gemmy churnings of hummingbird
or maybe a
charmer of a nightingale or two —
or their
remains, leavings, really — but
birds
weren't the point. She
stuck

flecks of broken jewelry — a sliver finding,
an emerald
glass cabochon, a tiny track of
seed pearls
and garnets — trailing like breadcrumbs
to some
cottage in a fairy tale — as if they were
leading to
or away from some actual place
that lived
beneath the feathers. But this
didn't seem
right: she wanted no precision, no
tapering
ley lines charting undercurrents so
she botched
the jewels, smearing pools
of
blue-green paint — a paste of oil and chalk —
and maybe
she should grind up some of those
winkles
over there in the tide-line, stomping
them into a
gray-pink haze; she could name
the piece
shell-shocked; or, if she guts that carcass
of plover,
or just tears off a kelpy wing of gull,
she could
call it a wing and a prayer.

Cora Goes Birding

This was a bad idea.
The creepers in this marsh are thick
with secret whispers; they stick
together, resenting intrusions. They
flick their slick fronds, ensnaring
unsure ankles and muddying
the mazy path. She is after
Red-necked grebes and Glaucous gulls,
Least Terns, Warbling Vireos, godwits,
Merlins, Ruffs, or whimbrels, though
in a pinch, a Green-winged Teal or
simple purple finch will have to do.
Or, something called a Bufflehead,
or a Common Goldeneye, though
it's baffling that anything
with golden eyes could be
considered common. She once
saw a girl with golden eyes — or, really,
a strange perplexing amber or
maybe just a trick
of the wayward autumn haze. A fall
here would be risky, the muck quick
to suck at clumsy knees and shins.
She could get stuck here overnight,
shivering among the sedge and stalks
while flustered snowy egrets
menace her from trees. She sees
an osprey loop and glide with
elegant unhurried ease, then balk,
and bank at her proximity,
and gyre toward a distant perch.
Whatever else she's done today,
she is oddly gratified to say that
she's been eyeballed by a bird of prey,

she's made without a clear demand,
a hawk re-swoop
and change its plans.

Cora in the Woods

Glue
doesn't stick
to mossy
logs
so she is
at a loss.
Something
rough,
but smooth
enough
to use as
base
is wanting
so
she will
make
an
assemblage —
wanton and
shadowy
and sure to
be
knocked
down.

No, not a
frilly fairy house
with acorn
cups and stone tea tables,
pine needle
beds and blankets of fern,
berries on
birch bark plates,
offered to
sate a fluttery,

imperceptible
swarm of hunger.

No, no
fairies — though,
she is
momentarily taken by
the thought
of fairies crashing
into some
trompe l'oeil gap of
bolete cap;
not very nice,
the wisps
of stunned fairy
glinting
into puffs of gloom. She
could go on
about
smashing
fairies, bogus 'shrooms but
the sun is
intermittent and, again,
there's
nothing here to glue.

Cora in the Lane

A country
walk
sounds
tweedy, bracing, and
dusty as
old brogans.

She's
brought a sack
to stuff
with useful finds.

The early
light is delicate,
not too
sure of itself, a
little too
coy for her taste. She

prefers
definition today, not
this frail,
unmuscled, boneless
morning
imprecision.

What's all
this
sheepish
pink about? These
watery
licks of barely green?

Even the stones
seem hesitant,

peering
from the mud
like lost
or beaten dogs — those
black ones,
shiny like eyes, you see.

Hence, the
image. Of mutts. Longing
for laps or
attention. Naught but
pleas and
fleas. Now,
plucking a
few from the muck
she cannot
shake the image of the eyes,
and swears
she hears them blinking
as she bags
them,
stowed for
future mongrel visions.

Cora Goes to Market

Someone makes art out of cereal boxes.
This sounds good to her.
She, though, would like to make art
out of actual cereal
but she has to figure out a way
to varnish and preserve
the actual flakes and puffs.

In her crisper are radishes, mushrooms,
a bitten Bartlett pear, and parsley.
She has no
recollection of the parsley —
or if parsley is
edible at all — even when not
creepily aged and crisped
with freon frost.

Possibly, she was smitten with the parsley
when she glimpsed it in its open-air bin,
a slight sea-green breeze ruffling
its sweetly floozyish
deep green ruffles. Possibly
she poked and picked through heaps
of parsleys before this particular bunch
beckoned, like a fresh
kitten at the pound,
and nestled next to the artisanal cheddar
in her market basket, then swayed,
happily, eons ago, home.

This may have been the time of the recipes,
the book of fifties meals
heavy with must and someone else's labor,
a dinner companion for several
hearty, soup-ridden weeks.

She'd simmer whatever was to hand, prop
the book by her bowl
(cayenne- and saffron- hued glazed pottery;
sage scalloped placemat, old bone-handled cutlery)
and gaze moonily into the succulent past,
when cereal was used to coat chicken parts
and add crunch to breaded fried canned clams.

(This may explain the welter of unfamiliar cereals
accusing her from the doily-dolled-up shelves. And
may also explain the doilies.)

She'd slurp wistfully and wonder if
she ever
did anything with zest
and if she should buy
a zester.

Garnishes had
a chapter to themselves:
turnip roses, zucchini trees,
celery curls, tropical birds made of pods
and carrot bits with parsley plumage.
Parsley was a kitchen nudge, like brillo pads.
Parsley was tricked over meatloaf, turkey cutlets,
lamb shanks, and Wiener schnitzel. With
parsley, a gal could trust
her dish would make a show — like painting
with an easel, it meant, "I am no drudge;
I have resolve; I plan —"
nothing flicked together merely, with oddments
from some lazy cans. Even tuna casserole
became a feast with artful twirls of parsley.
It's possible that a little twitch
of nightly parsley, made some marriages
more efficient.

It also was a civilizing force. You'd have to pause
before shoveling in the fish sticks. You'd
have to think, "Aha, this is a meal
that was prepared, prepared with skill
for me." So parsley signaled love.

She'd lick her lips, which she had rubied, twist
her single strand of tidy pearls and
pretend to remember basting and buttering,
pounding translucent fillets and
the satisfying slither of mushroom soup
easing convenient taste
from the tin blades of its cranked open can.

The book is now all floury with remembrance.
She thinks she'll cut it up and pound it with a rolling pin
onto a small formica trash-recovered table
and decoupage the pages into
pleasant table-settings with sprigs of parsley
laminated in like fossils.
She'll call it, Forever Green.
Or I Remember Parsley.
Falsely.

Cora Alights

On a breezy, challenging day,
the gold light scuds against the mess
in her insignificant bedroom. She
accepts what dawn issues, arises, and
is gone, gathering gauntlets as she may.
Simmering before her coffee is a feckless
misanthropic light; moody and erstwhile is the
first light's gold. She sips the milky drama
of the light spooling in her coffee
as the morning, beset by villainous clouds,
vamps its veils and wiles itself free.
She whiles away the morning,
drinking the tiny puckers of softly lit rain
tepid in her coffee. The clouds, no longer
cast as scoundrels, fling their murk
in a kind of moorland mist;
Her stoop seems fraught
with heather. Clumps of ragged crabgrass
claw the brittle paving stones and
in the liminal light from her graying dreams
appear as daggers of crowberry. Soon
the clouds hunker down for a good
dense walloping of the heath. She
takes cover under a blistered awning, flicks
a pine needle from her mug, watches the
pinkish patio transform into purple miles of ling
and spiky tufts of yellow gorse, of course.
Then distant in the grubby sound of surf and seizing thunder
a lost voice hails salvation over the imminent bog
of her wandering need. She could have him call
"Cathy" but, as her coffee is damp with
fitful morning rain and discomfiture,
she wants
very much

to hear the avowal of the
drawn-out mournful vowels of
her own loved windswept name.

Cora Talks with Trees

The sea gave her bumptious pastel town what-for
and bashed the whimpering rose hips
with an oblivion of salt.
It was all sand and mayhem, and the roots
of every juniper scrabbled
for an arid patch of luck. She
pours anguish from
her kelpy garden boots and plucks
something fishy from the rills of mud
wormed into the shredded birdhouse.
Why such colossal brine didn't
keep the startled mums preserved...
she frets, recalling honey-hued,
prissy, pickled-looking faces.
The mums I hated, anyway. They
are only obligations. But there is
heartbreak in the strip of soil
blanched beneath the asphalt
pitched from her peaky roof.
You call yourself a gardener?
It is the dwarf Alberta spruce,
companion of her porch-warm days,
stoic bearer of cheery winter elves.
The voice rasps with brown accusing needles
like spittle on an out-thrust crag of chin.
She goes on the offensive, to fend off
memories of green and softer rains.
I never did. And what was I to do? I can't
restrain the tides. Couldn't
milk the ground of salt. Or dig
a surge-proof hidey-hole.
You are supposed to be hardy. I expected this of the figs.
She thinks she hears the spruce
rattle a final indulgent sough
as she flails, with the stump of a pitchfork,

intemperately, and vows
to implacable ash and elder
that none of it is her fault.

Cora Performs Her Art

Some constraints are in order,
some rules, a set of
clear restrictions or a code
that she can cannily apply
and even, subversively,
break

to force her random stroll
into a clever moving truth,
wittily ironic, droll
in an early summer, humid sort of way
since she will be all things:
maker, performer, witness, witless critic —
naturally, this takes a toll.

She spies a flap of fallen lily leaf,
a mangy dog-leash dripping from a mesh-link fence,
a rotting log, a little girl pressed against a window ledge —
so L becomes a rule — and randomness within the L
a goal — all surprise proximities fair game —
some L's are bound to stick, however strange. Now
she's on a roll.

Another rule is: now — so
lily, leaf, leash, and little girl
(do adjectives count? This must be sorted out.)
are null– like lines stricken from a
not-yet-written tome or ironic limerick.

Still, there is that backward glance — if she really
needs the ledge or little girl — (and
she'll reserve the right to adjectives
if there are no good L's forthcoming)
Land could count, if context need be sure and quick —
though land's in short supply and rather unspecific —

here are bitty plots of soil with flimsy fists of lilacs
trying to budge from scrappy looking bush — so
lilacs does it — there's a rush! — and hopping
like a bug across her path, a scrap
of balled up paper — a market list, in fact —
eggs, milk, chai tea, tofu, wheat bread, chick peas,
lemons — which poses a dilemma —
list, of course, can count — but lemons?
No lemons are at hand except the lemons of the mind.
A gift of fortune can't be slighted
so *I like luck* is how she ends her artwork.

Cora Resolves

To rid herself of girlish wonder
To eat more bananas
To be plain spoken
To carp less and be
more efficient. She
is often tired of hoping
for a breakthrough, a staid
wardrobe dark with ancient furs melding
into adventurous snows. Could
some bonanza of beguiling bide
in the fissure of an undiscovered stone?
Could this star-shaped freak of leaf-mold rising
from the pensive muddled January verge
indicate occult direction, a thin rent
in the dizzying shimmies of captivating veils?
She shapes mouths, momentous,
in the grit prickling the sludge
from a mediocre storm, and begs
to hear filamentous whispers
pulsing something numinous
but all she really hears are hisses
from her arms against her waxy slicker.

If angels did appear, they'd snicker,
flap celestial wings like chickens,
shoo her home to wash the dishes.

Spitting Image

Fractured, this image of a swan:
early morning, early June,
a slow sun ruffling the clouds
where they tend to their nest of storms.
Egrets watch, aloof familiars, from
the blighted coven of skeletal cedar
and red maple, dead, still reaching,
intricate with power.
And the cygnets rake coils in the green
stillness of the marsh, their mothers prodding
pondweed and stonewort, harrying the tadpoles.
There is a scrim of birch and alder, and more
herons skimming for snakes and fishing-spiders
as light curls and dabs haphazardly.
Lured by the hazy peace, I blunder
from my clumsy blind and venture
to a translucent verge, too flimsy to bar
my love-sick gazing.
An inch too far and I am beset by
an eruption of wing and hissing.
The egrets don't lift a feather to save me.

A Decided Loss of Steam

It's anybody's guess when I'll go,
that last fizz sucked from that pineal chakra
at the crown by God's indelicate straw. I
can see some sort of cosmic huff and puff,
spitting souls to the astral winds, a manic
inappropriate geyser of giggling
when a bit of ego-bubble bulges up the nose.

That's me, the clog in the nose of the Absolute.

There's something achieved: I would never have
mentioned a *nose* or possibly *sucked* heretofore.
Looky here: I'm jammed with ancient fire,
and can certainly say what I want
even if it means straddling a regressive twinge
of self-abasement in a venerably luminous dark.
Or if I am a liar.

I want to see
beyond the mortifying dread
into a bath of rare proximity, a kind of
underwater stellar song, rippling with real
density,
a spirit's twin in the galactic tub
washing the neck of my
urgently put-upon, hang-dog fear.

Let me be clear.

I've seen it all before without surprise and wouldn't mind
a sudden fit of shivering before the final dawn,
a kettle of kestrels swooping for lizards
in rain-bright swollen skies.

Great Mother, I've bungled all my chances.
Can I beg a few more tries?

I want fair weather for this final leg,
or, since fair is never fair — of course, old dog,
these tricks I know — I might depend on storms
to buoy me, or if not buoy, then transfix —
and if not that, then just desist
with any pretense of disaster and let the heavens rip.

Doll's head with Jetty and Plover

Pinched in slabs of limestone in the groyne:
barnacles, bladderwrack, blue mussels and,
winking in a tide pool, a fist-sized head
of blanched 1950's rubber.
Too small to be Helen, I shrug inanely,
Helen being my first doll-baby,
molded chestnut hair, chubby arms curved
in a permanent hug. *Love*,
I think, and try to pick her out,
an over-cooked quahog in a
frothing-over pot. She's held
by ropes of May weed and alaria,
her little neck filled with brine, small bones,
silt, and ancient air.
How old am I? The ache, swift and
muscle-stunning; I am stiff with
sudden fear and reckoning —
a piping plover too nearby is
only a pulse speeding into a glint
of someone else's memory
in someone else's eye.

Gingerbread Mix

So this year, penitent, I
bought a mix.
The requisite men were cut
and baked and
it all took under an hour, even
with waiting
for the rounds of dough
to chill. What is it with this
need to spice the air
with nutmeg, cinnamon, and dark
disavowal? Where is the reproof
and where the violation
of the old wives' from-scratch code?

Last year, the house fell down.
Gumdrops popped with seismic
imbecility and a farcical music-hall patter
held up my nerve. Something about
effort unwasted and
still being tasty and
togetherness being
the durable goal.
I could have bludgeoned
the idiot thing, its licorice shutters and
hedgerows of toffee
too garish and ambitious
for a simple bungalow.
Icing thick as avalanches — a
mountain resort's worth —
on the eaves.
Nothing would hold. Nothing
would withstand my clumsy
eagerness to please.
As if houses of cookies

could trump
houses of cards.

Pound cake, angel food, puddings, meringues, and
breads with a hint of cardamom —
There is, in my hurried resurrection of
kitchens of yore,
the fairy dust of sifted flour,
oleo and oats, the crisp dither of brown
sugar rasping golden oaths,
the whir of my mother's mixer,
the rim of a ceaseless day,
the untrammeled joy of licking
the bright and mystic blades.

Awake at Half-Past Three

Strapping on a shawl like a backpack, she
heaves into the dense thickets of the kitchen,
the usual moonlight wafting its ethereal charms,
which she is having none of. Glowering, she
flattens a tea bag with hunks of lemon and
settles down to ruminate despite the moon's upbraiding.
So and so is a so and so and why my aching back, wrist, eyes, and
    life?
Could I, she grips her steamy cup, dream up a spine for myself at
this late,
hard-boiled age? And then, who would be left to walk with
into the dappled mystery, with roses still to trim?
She posits a friend —
someone with pruning shears and a steady hand who still
can climb a hill without a gasp for feeble breath.
Someone who hasn't had a bypass.
Someone who still has legs that long
for wooded paths and craggy shores and nightly rounds
to latch the swollen shutters, chase the bats, steep the tea,
and help her
get a grip.

Sebago by Ice-Light

They told us the lake froze
with mid-winter regularity,
the ice thick enough to drive
a truck clear across
if you were thick enough to
want to. No one, to their knowledge,
ever tried. We were unsurprised,
each year angling for the same
droll, slow-spun reply as we
rented our September canoe.
Bobbing into our stride,
paddles swifting, we
reeled with the sweet allying
joke of it: each year
the same men, flannelled at
the same post, trolled
the same seasoned watery ghosts
and lifted certainty of ice
into the thinning autumn sun,
launching, unawares, our own
careless lolling season.

You snapped twigs for perpetual
kindling, stoked stones into giving
their sparks to your light-loving lens.
As the stars coved and spun,
reliably northern and dimensional,
I lay on the bedding I had fixed,
listening to the thwacks of your
lantern -lit axe and the human chuckles
of the ducks in the soft unsleeping waves.

Each year we said we'd winter there,
camping with unassailable gear
and fearless Yankee brio. We

would discover the truth of the freeze,
unsnarl our workaday distractions
and maze through the drifting woods,
tracing tracks of 'coon and un-denned fox
and, braced and booted, traipse
mid-lake to the mystical pine islands
to which we had rowed recurrently
in the days when our seasons
still seemed warm enough
and certain.

Book Review for *Divertimento for the Clear Light of Morning:*
An All-Consuming, Occasional Memoir

The theme of defilement is unnervingly
unmistakable in these pages,
haunted as they are by the spirit of omission.
The author's admissions are
astonishing in their
painfully haughty disregard
of the practical symmetry of
reader/writer noblesse oblige. One gives,
the other gives more. Here, both reader and
writer are on equal footing — a kind of literary
egalitarian snobbery that denudes
these wildered thickets of their ghosts and
winter berries. It's a cold climate, despite the
musicality and promised dawn of the title.
I see little of clarity here. Far less of actual
diversion, and only an "occasional"
overwrought irony, a kind of hard-won,
enervated blink at an all-*consumptive,*
perilously lassitudinous,
depthless murk of a morning
I cannot, in good conscience,
wakefully recommend.

Book Review for *The Lost Harbor Dump, a Calculated Risk and Mystery*

The author must be familiar with junk, the details are
so variously concrete and ephemeral, but in a solidly ruinous,
ethereally grandiose way, the dimensionality of loss is
superbly rendered, knowingly, intimately, in a kind of menacingly
bland ministry of attrition. *That's how it is in the dump*, the author
seems to say, convincing us to put on our mental hip boots and take
a slog through the leavings. And, of course, the leavings are our own.
The author is particularly adept at demonstrating through the untidy,
oftentimes revolting but ever-panoramic ragged edges of the form,
the dagger-like shards of our own smashed mirrors, our own seven
or more years of unadulterated ill-luck. *It doesn't get better*, the author
seems to say. *Watch your footing, though you might, you'll never,*
and I mean
never
find a worthy keepsake, and you'll sure as hell not
find your way. Which makes for murky, though reliably
prismatic, at times, going, as if the charge were worth the
inevitable witness to incineration or pestilent deflation. It
is a good enough read, though, sodden with a, perhaps dubious,
fascination with the wormholes of aspiration and
is oftentimes tetchy and even a good bit preachy
with its relentlessly strewn images (mold and paper-char
like graveclothes clawed by the finger-like lids
of ancient canned hams)
of the impacted, faded discards
of unavailing effort.

Astral Endorsement: Discarded Words

I. Didn't make it into the novel

astral (endorsement)
(Restrain restore degeneracy attunement abasement)
(indelicate/bounced) (to the present tense)
(store) (less wrenching) (maneuver) (relative) (self-reliance) (years in
NY) —
Overshadow (glaringly) (one-note). (keeps the flame), [adjective/verb
    mix?]
[lost] [exclude myself from]
[inviting] (no). [to safety] (no).
[softly] stitched (hatched) (devotion) (texture) (x)
But I must say that those years were a most propitious time to come
    of age in.
[propitious imprudent cant synthetic]
[snakily edenic]
hazarding/nostrum/crackpot/Gehenna

II. The novel didn't make it

(reactive chi)/ (rusty sentiment)
(deliberately accumulated)scanty/Aesopian/Aesopic (x)
parlous/venturous/westward/devotionalize/
spiritual tightrope/varied thrush
Tangram/runaway/dappled (no).
Stowed away on his own visions/adumbrate/fey
(chamelion /salamander laugh — a laugh whose register depended
    on who was in the room.)
(a pack of plucky scouts)
He knew a calyx from a sepal
mortifies.flimflam/mobocracy.meliorate
Distracted wisdom
canny/concoction/crackpot/Gehenna

Misreading the Byline

Peycho, not Psycho.

I so wanted it to be Psycho but
it's only my dingy glasses, my sloppy eyesight,
my haste, my penchant for proofs of ironic
overstatement to collect for my ironically unmarked
case file. Had it been Psycho, I'd have
had something else to say: Who is this guy? A
suburban high school kid with biker gang pretensions?
Does he have tats snaking up his forearms, squeezing
a bug-eyed mongoose on his back — or, plunging into his
spine, a series of decorative daggers —
three-dimensional gristle and rusty beads of blood? Or
a bellicose stiletto over the eye, or, better yet, the heart,
with "mother" curled garishly onto the hilt? Does he, in fact, say "tats"?
And he must have real piercings — tongue, nipples, lobes, brow,
    snout —
safety pins are so passé, as are bolts and bars and plugs- but what is
    that about?
He'd thrust the sharp ends through his nares anyway and any other
    palely pinkish parts —
Perhaps he'd thread a thumb-sized phillips head or a scattering of
    steel-tipped darts
replete with turkey feathers into prominence, the renegade; perhaps
    he's only
crazed in fits and starts and never goes deranged full-tilt?

If I could order up a psycho, I'd have a pussy cat
who rocked and stared with arch command, a flick
of mayhem in his throat and spring bolt action in his glare.

You Couldn't Know

That your one good dress would be flotsam,
sixty years after you shimmied it over your
tentative hips and sashayed past your father
clutching closed the nubby wool of your
everyday coat with febrile nonchalance.
He, of course, eyed you with a vacant,
reflexively hostile suspicion,
one too many shots of Sambuca con la mosca
riddling him with petulant distraction,
ridding him of virile resolve. (That time
you and Annie snuck out to hear
"Shake that Thing" at the Cotton Club — You
made it as far as the stoop before the demitasse
cup cracked your skull and your audacity. Annie
was snagged by her soft, quivering, quellable curls). So
this time, no sneaking. He wouldn't believe
you'd dare once again. And that was how
you did it; you just did. You
stashed the coat on 104th behind the bins
at St. Lucy's, praying Madonna Mia
that the nuns wouldn't tip the trash,
especially that shifty old strega, Immacolata,
who jerks your wishes right out of your brain,
with her squinty glance and smirk.

Bead by bead, you stitched
a triumphant dazzle of defiance,
crystals, seed pearls, ruby, jet,
and golden specks of glass, thriftily filched,
bead by bead, from your nightly, eye-
straining job of threading with glitz or
delicacy, rich women's unreachable gowns.
Your own was a year in the making and still
the beads were scattershot in an angular thrust
of derision. No beauty, you refused the light-hearted

chiffon and went for the silk and the taffeta — a brazen
azure and black with those beads shot like arrows
over the heart and flirting wryly with the fringe
at the pronged, asymmetrical hem.

The story never proceeded beyond the ash cans
at St. Lucy's. So you are perpetually outwitting,
swinging up the street, rhinestone hair comb
catching the moony shimmer of the early
Harlem night, out-smirking Sister Immacolata,
though without the bitter residue of malice
on what would become an irregularly
sharp and sometimes reckless tongue.

After the flood, the dress drips
your glory into the murk and swirl
of the leavings in my cellar
as I lift it above
drowned volumes and
voluminous petticoats, bags of
letters and baggy stiff-legged jeans.
There is no escaping its staying power:
even in ruins, it is still unabashed, the least
bead clinging fast to the
blasted inches of slick disintegration,
the hitch of the uneven hem
unrepentant to the last.

Dead to Rights

I. Easter, 1951

You come from a place where pears seemed exotic
and the hoity toity rosemary prickling the spuds
stuck in teeth and craw. The roast needed naught
but salt and, in a pinch, some pepper. Never the muck
of *seasonings* daubing that good fat, Frenchifying the gravy
and tasting of pretension, rubbing the tongue
the wrong way home.

II. Christmas Eve, 1954

Can you stand your ground and serve the canapés,
your fervid apron strings goosing you
like pesty swats of ghostly winter winds?
The baby crinkles dreams in the sharp sheets,
scrabbling for colored lights and the smells
of peppermint and pine.
You check and smooth and leave
the oven on full throttle,
killing the chill from the goose.
You check and smooth and leave
the drippings from the brown sauce
on the regal sheen of your shirtwaist's gold charmeuse.

Spindly carols wheedle boozily,
sly with gin and tinsel, trying to buy off sins.
The baby is passed around and cooed to flopping chins.
Midnight tears glint ancestries of snow
and far-flung long ways home with farther still to go.

You shake shiny for-the-road cocktails,
rummage for your nerve
through fallen drifts of hypertensive tissue,
strangleholds of stringy light

and gobs of too-bright bow
oozing green beneath the glow
of ornamental grievances
and draggles of old news.
The baby slackens, gutters out.
It's time for you to choose.

III. Easter, 1964

Arise, men on the porch.
Release your crowded beers
as if they were balloons about to sprint
into the resurrected air.
Your daughter, barreling through on back-chat
and chocolate, lobs a painted egg,
at the paper mache chicken's head.
The bonnet cracks from side to side
and whacks an heirloom egg,
all sugared intricacy and purple lamentation
spilling like charms in a fine, belated mist,
an exultation of flocks rushing like hilarity
from a fatally opened fist.

Incidental
(For Jessie)

I.

The world creases sometimes
less like the brittle page of an old paperback
(one with a moon on the cover — and the soft
eyes of a girl peeking over a mess of creepers riddling
through a neat fringe of boxwood)
and more like a bed sheet busy with violets and snow drops
slept on fitfully and dragged into a stealthy dream of
a constant hand, smoothing, rumpling, smoothing.

II.

Settling: sediment, plans, down, for less —
and sometimes a disaster comes snuffling
through the startled dawn and the troubled
trees close ranks, flimsy wings shuddering with
whatever ways the winds blow.

III.

Times being what they always are — delicate,
ponderous, no-account, pressed — there
must be will, decrees, assertion — just
to keep the fireflies brave enough to burn.

Stakes

Wendy isn't budging
from the sill. The moonlight
is all hype and the shadows
cling like dirty sorrows, already
dragged through the years.
The boys knock heads in their fever
to burst wanton through the briny spheres,
steering by the spill and angle of the portent
of her tears.

It's sinisterly clear
that no one's going anywhere
without hitching their hurried wingspans
to the power of her will.

That fairy, tedious blur of ire,
splitting hairs in the corner
gives her the creeps.

Someone's bound
to slough a shadow, lose direction,
air a grievance, grub a story,
get a wind burn, irk a pirate,
beg belief, and
play for keeps.

Hokey Goddess

I. Flea Market Find

There was a chance that she was real.
And so, I lugged her, hugged her rough
stone belly to my own, and listed
toward the banal enlightenment of the cash box.
"Oh, you've found my lady," said the lady
who was keeper of the books.
I palmed my change and glanced stonily into her stare,
tensing for the story of a market in Peru or
an art fair in the city, or a garden gone to extravagant seed
and blessed with fecund celebration once the
statue drew the birds. "Crone," instead, she whispered.
Her hair was white beneath a hat of tattered straw,
a mess of downy newborns upended from a hasty nest;
her eyes were steady blue, not piercing, just unwavering.
I pretended to mis-hear, the safer route, yet all that speculation.
I itched to hiss: "Who are you calling crone, you hag!"
and to shove her backwards into the doddering camp table
teetering with old delicacy: tea cups, decanters,
china girls with poodles chained to wrists,
gemmy bottles gleeful and smirking
in the midmorning patches of mid-summer sun.
With befuddling force, this instant gall swerved
to the curb of my teeth, just missing
a misanthropic lurch into the
hum of an unsuspecting air.
Everywhere summer but here?
I inched away,
gulping mealy mouthed imprecations,
my arms achingly full of ambiguous stone.

II. Brought Home

Of course, it was crone at first sight.
Adrift in recognition, I set my goddess of the flea

in a tiny gale of late beach roses,
in my windswept patchwork garden
by the late September sea.

III. Crone Consciousness

Those blue eyes are hard to escape. I expect,
when I drive around this picturesquely seedy coastal town,
to spy her sweeping a crumbling stoop
or flinging seed into the dreary snow,
white hair still clinging to a brim of durable straw.

The truth is, I want an old lady —
older still than I —
vaguely nautical with
an incongruous woodsy air
of cloistered creakiness —
to see what I can't ever see —
the abandoned
ship of prayer
on this grim and lowering sea.

IV. Come Home.

Foolish, I lean into the briars, ostensibly to weed.
"Crone."
Lithic, distinctly blue-eyed, and not
the soughing of the non-existent wind.
When I notice enough to notice,
I feel the soil beneath my knees
and watch the tensile delicacy
of a web of my own thorn-caught
whitening hair.

The Accidental Garden

Why not just see what blooms?
After the storm hurled the mad sea
onto the already flimsy promise
of my wanton, low-rent garden —
I watched the salted iris twitch, the lilac spit foam,
the English ivy gag on twisted iron stakes
sagging on crumbled, chalk-faced gnomes.
The stalwart pines frizzled rustily
like the husks of trampled honey bees
in an overheated ransacked hive.
Nothing was alive, not one speck
of rue or rosemary, breath of stunned
beach rose bud or shiver of beleaguered knotgrass.

The neighbors went to town, hauling bags of gypsum,
shoveling stalks, snapping branches, sweeping splintered pots —
re-seeding and replenishing, sending death spinning
while I retrieved a blistered Buddha
from the scrap heap at the curb,
let him bleach inside a wilderness of thistle
and waited for the winds to do their work
of wafting new beginnnings.

The Cure

A stranger,
in an unguarded moment,
at the bus-stop, say,
or on a ticket line for an early show, might
look a certain way and lift another's curse,
perhaps by distractedly worrying the tarnished clasp
of an efficient patent purse, or by rubbing a thumb to a crease
in a latently optimistic brow. Or there might be contact,
the kinetic static of surprise
shocking shy smiles from the pardons. And later,
as the dusk purples and replies in kind
to the dark beseeching of the city's footfalls,
there might be among the hurly fray
a movement less resigned and less inured,
and more buoyantly far-reaching.

On the Boulevard: *L.A. 1975*

On the Boulevard,
a trippy little ghost
springs forth on cork-soled shoes,
hugging a parcel of pernod and pretzel rods, and
a heap of dirty clothes,
a gleam of arty slyness, practiced
in a mirror, hovering mistily,
as if drawn about her mouth
with a crush of fuchsia gloss.

She works in a bookstore.
She adopts a cat.
The air is dingy where she sleeps.
The pillow case and bed linens
jolt their besotted
orange flowers
creepily into her dreams.
Thin bugs crawl in the cupboards
and the cat begins to stink.
It will not hug her or let itself be
groomed. It does not seem to like
the taste of its own fur.

On the Boulevard, a heavy-jawed man,
tips over cartons and plies the paper bags.
She leaves offerings of peanut butter
on soft white bread, apples, and cans of
orange soda. She never knows if he finds them.

The bookstore owner stalks her, fixes her
with parroty beak and eyes, refuses to pay
for her many hours stocking shelves and
dodging his fulsome innuendo.
She snaps the cat into a cage and swings it to
a shelter. A new friend/co-worker helps her trap it

with cushions and bath towels. It looks at her
with predatory disdain,
hisses, then silently claws the bars.

On the Boulevard there is a dress shop where
singing acts and dancers buy their audition garb.

She hands them their red boas and silver sheathes,
keeps guard over the dressing room: no thieves, no
men dressed as women, no hanky panky,
no nefarious deals. She
is an unlikely security force. She often lets in the men
since they are mostly indistinguishable from the women
and she is too polite to question their gender and intentions.
A small green dress made of silken handkerchiefs, a motley paisley
shawl, tinted like trampled daffodils in mud, many pairs of beaded
earrings, gossamer head wraps, pendants with tiny shells and coven
symbols all disappear on her watch. She sweeps her long hair
across her thin shoulders and upbraids her latest date, chattily,
to her new girlfriend/co-worker. She
won't take his money. She is woefully feckless and disinterested.
She pivots like a jewelry box ballerina, sees
him standing there, hands shoved into his pockets, straining
to smile. He moves lithely toward her, coldly lifts her hair, lets
it thud softly against her frail backbone.

A waitress drops a slice of paper on her plate.
A phone number unfurls like a fortune in a cookie.
A stocky man with fly-away hair, colored like a ginger tabby,
grins invitingly as a rubber death's head. There is no metaphor
for how he implores and salivates, while dabbing the
grease from his chin. Her girlfriend/co-worker
whispers his name, his title, his affiliations —
translates him into dollars and gifts. He
expects to command, to conduct an easy business.
She drops coins into a callbox on the Boulevard.
A shadow whoops, another howls. Something sly inches closer,

something grubby frets gauntly near her hand. She whispers a plea
into the miles, stretching the shakes out of her voice with
the long sigh of her need. She doesn't want a red fleece robe. She

doesn't want another surprise box of cookies and noodle soups.
She doesn't want news: her little sister's play, her brother's baseball
    game,
the dog's near-brush with a neighbor boy's scooter. She wants
the kind of salvation that only comes with never having been
to the Boulevard in the first place.
There is going home.
But there is no turning back.

acknowledgments

"The Language of Little Girls," "Malady/The Glory of Little Girls," *Memoir (and)*; "The Terrible Miss Terrell," "In Kitty Liffey's Bar and Grill," "204th Street: Almond Cake," *Hoboeye*; "Foodstuffs," *Red Line Review*; "The Poetics of Character: Solitude and Attention," *Literary Mama*; "Antiphon," *Big Pond Rumour*; "Girls Girls Girls," *Volume* and *What the Sea Washes Up* (Dancing Girl Press); "Matty and Hatty and the L-Seven Marauders, or Wooly Bully in the Moonlight," *Umbrella*; "Alice and Red at the O.K. Corral," "Running with Wolves," "Stakes," *The Yellow Medicine Review*; "Notes for a Ghost Poem," *Subliminal Interiors*; "Ghost Poem," *OVS*; "Spitting Image," *Saxifrage*; "A Decided Loss of Steam," *Prick of the Spindle*; "Sebago by Ice-Light," *Aroostook Review*; "The Cure," *Shot Glass Journal*; "Astral Endorsement: Discarded Words," *Shuf Poetry*; The Language of Little Girls: Doll Babies," *Revival Literary Journal*; "Doll's Head with Jetty and Plover," *Turbulence*; "Gingerbread Mix," *The Mom Egg*;"Cora Talks With Trees," *The Stony Thursday Book (Limerick Arts Council)*; "Cora Goes Birding," *Plume*; "On the Boulevard" and "Thompson Street," *Cities: A Book of Poems* (Chuffed Buff Books) and "On the Boulevard" and "Incidental," *Morning Constitutional in Sunhat and Bolero* (Green Fuse Poetic Arts); "Hokey Goddess," *Journey to Crone: A Book of Poems* (Chuffed Buff Books).

42250847R00066

Made in the USA
San Bernardino, CA
29 November 2016